I0571664

Judge's Citation

Habitual Prayer seems like a fitting and off title all at once. Sure, these poems indeed are imbued with all the power, intention, mystery, and beauty of prayer, but nothing is habitual, routine, or ordinary about how this poet approaches language. From a poem where "too many dahlias/grow taller than angels" to another that proclaims "I expect blood when/I crack open the softening door," again and again in this brief and stunning collection I found myself tripping over language so fresh and wise, at times ancient and at times from electric dreamy future, making new all the places we poets have looked to find our work: into death, into the garden, towards love, and into the mirror. *Habitual Prayer* has made me a fan of this poet's magic, how they transfigure language into these precise, lush spells and invocations that unsettle me so. The greedy prayer I cast out to my gods: please, please, more of this, more from this poet.

—**Danez Smith**, author of four collections, most recently *Bluff.* For their work, Danez has won The Forward Prize for Best Collection and been a finalist for the National Book Award and the National Book Critic Circle Award.

Praise for HABITUAL PRAYER

In Ava Chen's *Habitual Prayer*, the "I" speaks but is not the subject. Its voices sound like people who've made listening an art. Each appeal is both intelligent and heart-forward, generously including an entire world in a single poem, sometimes a line. I'm inspired by the gentleness of these voices, how they highlight a thought or image and let it go without resistance, allowing the next moment to happen, and how tenderly they address the you in each poem. *Habitual Prayer* writes toward a love so steady I'm left with new possibilities of what poetry can provide: "a soft universe of our own."

—**K. Iver**, author of *Short Film Starring My Beloved's Red Bronco*

Chen's writing feels like the best kind of dream—vivid and surreal all at once, full of lines that transcends all bounds of the page. *Habitual Prayer* paints life as a constellation of wings and lightning, of "glass lungs" and "fishnet throat" slipping and surviving. "In these spaces between/going & leaving, briefly/I am unable to die," Chen writes, constantly drawing out the small, impossible truths of what is holy in our world. Reverent and intensely reactive, *Habitual Prayer* crystallizes expansive form, exquisite emotion, and Chen's distinctive voice into declaration and song.

—**Ivi Hua**, author of *Body, Dissected* (kith books, 2024)

Ava Chen's *Habitual Prayer* is at once kaleidoscopic and keenly focused. Each poem is dioramic, a reenactment of scenes domestic and private, a museum of small griefs and loves. Reading this book, I felt that "briefly/I [was] unable to die."

—**Jenna Nesky**

Winner of the 2023 Palette Poetry Chapbook Prize

Habitual Prayer

Ava Chen

RED MARE
PRESS

This is a work of fiction. Names, characters, places, and incidents are either the product of the author's imagination or are used fictitiously, and any resemblance to actual persons, establishments, events, or locales is entirely coincidental.

HABITUAL PRAYER

Copyright © Ava Chen, 2024. A Red Mare Press book.

Published in partnership with *Palette Poetry*, an online literary journal.

All rights reserved.

No part of this publication may be reproduced or reprinted without prior written permission of *Palette Poetry*. To inquire about rights and reprint permissions, please contact *Palette Poetry*.
www.palettepoetry.com / contact@palettepoetry.com

Red Mare Press upholds the right to free expression and recognizes the importance of copyright in fostering creativity. Copyright exists to inspire writers and artists to produce works that contribute to and shape our culture.

Edited by Marcella Haddad.

Cover design by Emelie Mano.

Interior design by Julianne Johnson.

Cover Art Attribution: Ava Chen.

Red Mare Press / Discover New Art, LLC
70 SW Century Drive, Suite 100442, Bend, Oregon 97702

www.redmarepress.com

Red Mare Press is a division of Discover New Art, LLC.
The Red Mare Press name and logo are trademarks of Discover New Art, LLC.
The publisher is not responsible for websites (or their content) that are not owned by the publisher.

ISBN 979-8-9901838-2-7

Printed in the United States of America.

Contents

Self Portrait as Fraying Seams

I was born at 11:11 a.m. though
        I didn't believe my mother
                for too little time.
How many times have I told you,
        she said, exasperated.
                How many times.
At age 5, I developed a sensitivity
        to the color of the ceiling.
                Mother's headboard
was a mirror: I sat like a fossil,
        studying my own wet skin.
                In middle school,
I gave a speech about middle school,
        ran out of unused names
                halfway through,
so I started piercing holes in my tongue.
        For years, a museum
                of destructive habits—
plucked leg hairs, sleeping on a cliff—
        has begged to stay original.
                The heel of my hand
presses into my eye to see better,
        as if they are held, not kept
                in the skull,
and would roll away like a soccer ball
        at the lip of a forest.
                I wear my contacts
once every week at best,
        every time I leave the house
                at worst.
I lost the ability to form habits in 2017
        when I drove past my old home
                and the inhabiting hag
had hung two green lanterns
        flanking the door.
                It was June.

It was a day I had forgotten
            my glasses and left hand,
                    and the fog on the window
couldn't get any brighter.

They Built the Power Lines Too Close

my physics teacher says,
they knew because of the ten cormorant corpses
they found below. It must have been
lovely, mouth stretched wingtip to wingtip

crying so sharp tears forgot skin,
fell through bones like water
filling the bird's eye into a bull—
waiting to be bloodied. I am flayed

by no language of ruin
and like how a nocked gun bruises a shoulder,
feathers burst, char in nature. But they've
leapt too far from their mother,

so ashes only season the coming winter,
when every dead thing has already been
swept into barrels. The ground's too hot today
for graves to be any good.

They tried moving the poles farther apart,
but cormorants kept piling.
This is because wires with current flowing
in the same direction attract each other.

An embrace formed from physics
is not an embrace at all. Lightning—
the only road made of traveler.
Wings—a cruel aphrodisiac.

Spleen curls into spark. A scar
envelops itself into oblivion.
Only a stranger's child should tell
a mother to close her eyes,

slick with the remains of a family
she can't understand. The eggs vaporize

like the organs, crushed thought a white
so mortal everything else blinds—

clouds, a daughter's gasping beak, damp grass.
Nobody turns as a pen thuds.
Somewhere outside a physics classroom
a plane shivers into a cormorant flock.

What's left composes, decomposes,
unbearably distinct against the horizon.

Ars Poetica as Childhood Bedroom

a contrapuntal

I start all my poems on laptops with fraying cables
                 because what is art without potential destruction?
because the last time I cried, the handheld mirror
                 turned to its wayward face and
gifted me anything but my grief: ceiling dust
                 shaken from moving out earlier, the window
that refused to stay quiet. the world that
                 burst inside. all the lights on and still I
cannot tell my hands from the chipped desk: both
                 wear skin like damage, frozen
in indecision and wedlock.
                 in a warning rougher than stripped wallpaper.
my wife texts me she can no longer digest and
                 I start writing laundry lists instead of poems:
every hour, a different omen goes numb:
                 my nondominant wrist, a flickering eyelid,
the pen snapped beneath
                 a chair leg. The seams of my jeans cave into
pockets filled with stolen birth certificates.
                 envelopes for unwritten redemption letters.
I heard detachment is a psychological phenomenon
                 but the screen flickers and I cough up baby teeth.
so I origami the dark into termination myths and
                 they fall like parachutes instead of paper cranes.
I chew the oxygen from clouds—
                 vacuuming the safety of my reflection.
I realize I am so still I have aged
                 two rooms over—cataracts float like toy warships
across my vision. a plastic star
                 plastered above, fissuring the ceiling,
seems to disappear each time I switch off the lamp:
                 a reminder of evolution. to curl up
at the bedside, I tell myself, years heaving
                 in nausea, is to swallow language and spit
out a cardboard shield, remember how
                 to beg. from my father I learned how

to diary without blistering. from my fingers
                        prayers slough off clipped nails:
I have forgotten how to keep myself holy.
                        but today, the portraits are no longer crooked.
too many colors are missing from the artbox.
                        motorcycles whine outside, siren-like. secondhand
smoke wafts in and out.
                        sparks and my names escape
from their refuge in my lung,
                        the tasseled curtain still billowing—
fairy tales peeling like paint—
                        searching for a larger body to seclude or invade.

For Now

after Avery Yoder-Wells / Grace Q. Song

In fog, sun is
everywhere, unsure.

In my garden,
too many dahlias

grow taller
than angels.

I scratch each thin shadow
off my thigh.

I have run out of water
& time

so I swallow a compass,
let my lungs spin life

back into breath.
I wait for the sun

to rise or set
in photographed twilight.

I fish the same pennies
from my stone fountain,

remember them
when they disappear.

Like any reflection
I do not break,

only multiply.
Each limb

a smaller
& older god.

Each god
a kinder alchemy.

My house grows
so warm or lonely

all the doors open.
I pass all the trains

until they resurface
ahead of me,

parting the sky
like wings.

I hoard bright sounds
in my eye

the way
a fountain hoards

its own blood.
In these spaces between

going & *leaving*, briefly
I am unable to die.

Allegory for Many Endings

a contrapuntal

in the corner, mother
stitches eyes onto each scarf,
azure, bamboo, hazel.
rocking delicately,
her bones slipping
between the wooden slats.
the sun spreads like a pelt on the carpet.
she skins the light, efficient.
wears it as her own.
this is a survival chore.
she inverts headlights
and keeps scars as hostages.
the fabric grows on the years,
putting every zodiac to shame
and forgetting that
seven marriages and nameless children
embrace, tighter
than tassels pushing out
her daughters' eyes and ears,
wool hollowing into love letters.
words into desire.
the radioactivity between *had* and *has*.
the light gutters, as if

peels shadows from the wall and
christens each her daughter—
against the fissuring plaster she's
at a thinning angle,
like starved fish through a net. she's fallen
through the blinds,
in this museum of silent bodies
mother wears anything dead like a trophy.
when guilt stirs she tells herself:
the most missed will become unrecognizable.
into unbearable lenses backlit by grief,
mother peers, refuses to blink.
each cuckoo nest destroyed,
for how light their futures weigh,
only the stillborn survive.
wrapped in stitched bathtub curtains
like a power line around a pine. brighter
where teeth used to sprout. mother searches
yet finds her own hands aged.
ash-caked ghosts stretching
desire into negative space like
when she passes between rooms,
she is alive.

Homecoming

I never thought returning would be like this: hair in the curler
            burning to dream.   cigarette stains blooming to your lip,
                    an injury for mother to scribble   on kindling
            & compensate in memory.   again the turntable brings
fish hearts   salted skeletons   anything   but water   to my mouth,
        temple drenched in sweat   I can taste but never know.
                    during dinner, beer-bellied uncles discuss
            dead countries   the economy
of a home, how nobody left but   all the windows opened
            as if flooded   all the lightbulbs blue-   hot to touch
                & through my bad eyes,   you're any   body
        with glass lungs.   children will remember anything
but the bed they first cried in.   opaque walls the worst
        & best weapon.   the sky craters like mother's tongue
                when she waves us out the last time
        & I learn how to christen everything   a relative of grief:
the dawn lifting to let shipfuls of traitors through   burnt salt
        my name sewed into a blind fish's body.   at the lake,
                two mirages surface: your closing eyes
        & the elegy I excavate   from between them, carve into
my fishnet throat—   in the thinning ink   there are only blades.
        basic   violence. into the wake we are
                    defocused prey   slinking into the tripwire horizon,
            never beyond—   in desperation
I throw open the curtains   & light floods in   to blind.
        I chip each portrait off the walls.   older gazes.
                younger deaths.   stale air hissing,
        a thief not realizing she's already in everyone's purses
and throats.   prayers whistle too far   for stars to recognize
        as prayers.   hair in my mouth   searching
                for a whiter place to invade.
        yet the waves are rising   still—   in haste I leave
bayberry pits in my throat   inkblots in the sink   an effigy
            instead of angel to man   the city,   a faulty panopticon
                from which   too many eyeless daughters
        will escape   with oil   flooding their lips.
afterwards, I get in the car   & watch   the house evaporate
        like smoke after a gunshot.   & blistering in surrender,

                    we are children translucent enough   to hold
         but not keep   we seeds sowed on burning highways
we fists that hurt deepest   into the earth
         we are made of.   the saltwater on my shirt
                    rogue planets.   galaxies of heritage   & other detritus.
         I scalpel home into casket   & casket into scripture
because only gods appreciate   reminders of amputation:
         breath bruising the getaway window   *hotel* fogged to *hostile*
                    the air so thick   I could trace its   sins   saints
         so bright I reincarnate   with scars still etching my tongue.
because mother, you know this best: we were never good
         at saving anything   that once belonged
                    to our bodies.

Of the Breathing Land

I pick a point and imagine a past.
Water rushing in, the edge
of an eye. I wish the damage
had stayed onshore—

too dry for atrophy
and too pragmatic for death.
For the dyslexic reader:
The man makes it out.

His glasses don't.
I want to unstitch my ears
but then the water will explode out—
the way a diamond ring

shatters hardest against itself.
This is how he overturned, too,
ocean rushing up in supplication.
I ask useless questions like

what color was the water
when it pushed out of your bones?
The rays as they burst
through your throat?

Standing on the pier, his mother
thought the back of his boat
was the back of a whale.
Everybody stayed silent

at first, until they realized
there are no whales
in the lake, nor ripples.
I will stop counting the waves

when my swelling throat calms
but whenever my finger touches
its surface a ringstain ripples out,
and somewhere, physics

keeps a body bobbing for breath, limbs
splitting or suturing the horizon
into bodies or points
refusing to focus

Apathy

A dream sighs into liquid on the hardwood.
Apathy fists the watery skeleton, fastens it
at his neck, feels the dream seep into the nape.
Spoils of a good run.   There are not enough
wounds in the walls for sunlight to reach in,
so Apathy paints the floors white instead.
Outside, leaves are falling, and do not crackle
under passing steps,   only blur.
There isn't much sympathy for the half-alive.
A flaming rock splatters across the sky.
A body descends from a tree
and forgets why scrapes form unreadable
epitaphs on its arms,   Apathy's back
facing the window. An armor of dust
on the wrong side of his coat. He observes
the body's limbs into branches, the rising chest
into wind swelling   beneath leaves.
When scenery stops changing for long enough,
the observer becomes the magician instead—
turning bodies into fossils, backdrops into foci—
because there is nothing about the truly dead
that we do not want,   or cannot be,
                    transformed.

Eulogy for the Unnamed Wound(er)

When I was three, I learned my first language from the warnings
printed on my crib. Later, I learned to lie when you twisted cigarettes

into my pale wrists & called them stars. Your voice spoiled
into wine in my mouth before I ever tasted the dead.

Two homes passed. In the hospital I gripped your hand,
warm as a mask, the way a daughter doesn't touch a heart

but the skin around it. Your eyes roved like trapped fish.
I pried your fingers from mine & you gestured, wild,

as if warding the wrong god away or beckoning the gurney-
white sun. To still or explode, I still don't know. This is not an elegy

but the dark space between its jaws. Saltstung. Teething.
At each dinner table I remembered to swallow the fish bones, too,

from your voice rattling like a dried needle, inhospitable blue.
Against each wall I watched shadows kindle patterns—

ars poetica shit—but I have not whittled my lungs enough
to feel any burning. I scratched my scalp seven springs deep

only to find an alphabet of echoes. I mistook the pocketknife
under my pillow for reinvention myths. All this to say:

I have never learned to erase scars without scarring.
I have chased redemption's glint for so long

it lights the back of my spine like a fuse, not a god.
A dandelion grown in the wrong orientation crawls into

the soil, seeking reasons for growth. Just like that—
a scalpel is not enough breath & fans the body

into flame instead, your heaving stomach drenched in pleas
pretending to be prayers. Afterwards, let dandelions

burst through your sockets. Hold your cold knuckles
against the sky as if color is not imaginary,

watch light splay into scalpels on our limbs.
Briefly indulge in these smaller deaths.

Reopen a wound too late & watch it
become the skin itself.

Dorm

Stains distort across the mattress as if blood rose
to pressure the foam, reminding it of mortality.
Here, the only stars are sunflower seed shells
stuck in the desk's wooden grain, contouring
the hands of time like scarecrows: brighter
and stiller than anything that once knew
how to die. In a diary left in a thunderstorm
words slam into each other, lustrous
and effortless enough to make loss
seem habitual, thus necessary.
The curtains sway before a closed window
with a broken latch. I sweep my foot
across the floor, catching clotted
and unclotted dust, various carcasses
still here after the seventh vacuum.
Like the rain fissuring pages into flesh
this light changes already marred surfaces
into artifacts that still wish for evidence
of closure. For now, the colors jostle,
restless, waiting for outside to darken first.
I can't remember anything about the door,
only the angling shadow after it opens like a blade—

Lodi

We bruise through a field, all thick weed and misplaced razors,
        tears scattered like seeds in the backwater.

Of the shapeless distances, you talk up trees
        like mythical debris. There's the haunted rifle

and handler, Amish mottled bull, a raccoon
        roasted on a spit. A vulgar metaphor for the moon.

From another world, a headlight scratches my thigh
        and I try to wipe it off. Fireflies blink perfect economies

of constellation, steeped against our skin like lasers.
        A bareback wind. A sophonic wisdom. A liquid

mirror. An echo with no wall
        crying and crying for a beautiful hunter.

The hunter is us. The air is howling, impatient. The article
        for *girl* and *grass* is *blade*. We swallow each sound,

heavy moons chafing throat to pearl.
        This is where rogue orphans of hope

take refuge, gleeful in their decay,
        burrowing in the ears of hapless souls.

This dream has no room for memory
        nor the madness of animals unclaimed—

        so we clench fireflies

    in our molars   crashing through brush
        unrelenting   twin stains

    in an oversaturated night
        sprinting over a translucent manhole

skimming the meniscus   light as severance
            our illegal eyes

spilling into   the sleepless and unheld
            spilling from the unholy frame

and the echo is unknown, oh
            it has to be—

turgid ground   facefuls of space
        rippling   horizon unclasping

unpainting   scars cracking on an endless palm
            our ripped smile

swelling beneath the lilt
            between chasing and being chased—

and we're sprawled   two soft shells
            sloshing in the lowest darkness   tragic

so grinning.   Torn
            from every unrusted machine

and free as any insect.

Overhead, aliens have eerily even luck in poker
        and veer off course, zip by Earth,

a comet brighter than blood. You see them
        and almost tell me.

In the middle of a forest, a tree thuds.
        A shard of sky slices your cheek—

you have broken the paradox
        yet no one else is grateful.

Behind, mushrooms crown through: baby fuzz,
        misting of a too-human thirst.

New wheat cleaves their ancestors into newer lumber.
        A tractor undulates dirt into gold.

A moonlit lip splits beyond the unblessed body.
        Where our limbs touch

countless unspoken languages root, flower into ginkgo.
        And then mothers call our names,

remembering them into finitude,
        hologramming us from ourselves

back into the dotlike houses and dotlike beds,
        so all night, I rub a wool blanket

into sparks of timelapsed stars:
        a soft universe of our own.

Elegy for the Dealer

A boy swallows what he's told are vitamins
               and fails out of calculus.
                         In a 7/11 parking lot
Ziploc bags exchange hands
               like quarters. A boy used
                     to swallow himself
into the moon, cratered
               with different names
                     for parts of the body:
eye an apple he carves
               a bowl out of,
                     stomach the flickering door
between hospital rooms,
               hand a blade sharpened into
                     a blade wound, skin
the color of a mirror:
               only reflecting the mother's
                     sorrow for a failed child.
The years scatter on the sidewalk
               like bits of leather caught between
                     animal and diary,
diary and deity
               peering through a wineglass
                     refracting a flatline
into the curves of a beating heart
               as if to say: something will
                     stop the truck.
Something will cradle sparks
               back into the sun.
                     Callouses used
to coat his speech, laden blue with
               alleyway promises,
                     the difference between
how every color of dirt makes dirt
               but every color of light
                     whitens into an unpaintable canvas:

the day before, the lamp
           had chiseled tiny wolves
                        into the hollow of his throat.
With a thumb
           he mothered the shadow
                        into splaying, but not enough—
as he lifted his hand
           a creature lifted into embryo into
                        the whine of tires splitting the horizon

Jamais Vu

I dip my palm into the water
and watch the seaweed you gifted me
bloat, brighten away. You reach down.
The knobs dimpling your back will evolve
into eyes. I burn, pregnant with salt.
The buoys slick with promises of surgery.

> I pass an apartment with
> shade undrawn, bodies kissing
> in and out of frame. Their shirts
> change colors with the angle.
> Light has become a habitual prayer,
> fickle and aimlessly devastating.

The holes in your jeans gape like mouths,
feeding on or drowning in the waves'
sulfur foam. Denim threads
like disintegrated teeth. Anemone
refracts into a beckon. I wade in.
I widen. We are all animals in our minds.

> In the right half of my eye,
> a blood vessel implodes.
> Only the world bloodies.
> I turn with the vulgar tide.
> Any smile could be a gunshot
> flashed hard enough.

Your spine melds back into your back
and the oracle halts. Face featureless
behind the lisp of a tumored landscape.
I turn memory like a spit,
eye over eye over eye as if wonder
is a thing to be manufactured.

> The lens swivels back. The shade gasps up
> before I touch it. Below, a man stepping
> soft as a spanked child too proud

to whimper. Night blurs and blurs
but I can still discern you from your body,
our reflection from the writhing sky.

I Have Loved You

As our steps align, I think this rhythm could have once snapped a bridge.
         The roadside grass yields for our feet,
blades turned so we cannot tell if they are bent or uprooted.
         A white tarp across the street makes a mountain
of a body. A CVS worker scrubs peroxide on the sidewalk
         bloodstain with the focus of a grave digger.
Nothing appears on the news—I have been checking for years.
         The stain seems to grow
closer to the road each time the worker stretches his neck, as if wanting
         a second death since nobody saw the first one,
or if they did, cried anything about it. But far enough away,
         covered tables at coffee shops
look like gurneys, spilled flasks like hit-and-runs. I wish us
         the same. I dig my fingers into the crease of your elbow
like a kid in a sandbox digging for gold.
         Tomorrow, near the stoplight, I will spot a black sheaf of hair.
I will cross the street before the car stops.
         But it won't be you, just another single mom with a covered stroller.
See, the constellations can't tell us who we are, or who
         we'll become, just give our fingers more excuses to trace the air
instead of each other.
         Tonight, the streetlights are broken—they know pity.
Silent and sprawled on the roadside grass,
         you could be mouthing prayers and I could be dry-
heaving with laughter or sobs beneath a fluttering tarp
         but in this invisible night, we'll never know anything, really.
In this life we only ever talk about beautiful
         strangers.

Angel's Landing

In the car, you point
to a gray truck
and call it
lumberjack green.
You've always loved anything
with room to dream.
We meet a girl
on the way up
with a month-fresh
pilot's license,
talk about how
the shittiest airline
to work in
is the easiest to join.
Wild things scatter
on the cliffside:
flowers bursting through
sediment loose or melted,
our jagged shadows
bubbling over
the rocks.
The black crescents
beneath my nails
wax into planets.
Cairns knock over
and reassemble
themselves.
I never look down.
I suppose angels
don't, either,
only marvel
at how beautiful
brief things are—
the rustle of an animal
running or crashing
through the underbrush,
the flash of sky

when you fell,
the blue so close
I could touch it

XX/XX/XXXX

We're sitting on the garden bench
smothered in snow, or seeds
the sky hid in its throat
and forgot to water.
You gave me your coat
because you couldn't stand
the smell of stale violence,
the meat of anything reflective
against your limbs.
The streetlights taxidermy your gaze
into nothing worth whispering over.
Everything's smaller and clearer
than I remember, clear as in moving,
not breathing—
as in your transparent body
which only exists in the pressure
my poetry exerts on you.
Space swallows itself into belief.
Fireflies get drunk off
the gold your hair sheds.
When you were seven,
you thought the moon
changed shape every night.
Tonight, wisdom
smears on the brick path,
warnings of a clearer
future. I leave it.
There is nothing more animal
than a dream, nothing
more still than a touch
deferred, nothing
more tragic than
all the fingerprints lost
by polishing memory's
vault.

Flood

Rain pounds the window
as if trying to enter, or escape.

It's a matter of perspective,
like all lies. Water fills

the hollow of my neck
into a mouth, or a grave.

Outside one's home or body
anyone can be nothing—

a compass buried in the rising mud
spins blindly not towards the future,

but towards its own iron frame.
I'm no different. I remember

every splintered fencepost
and uprooted weed

but never any of their names.
I expect blood when

I crack open the softening door—
I won't tell you what I find.

Acknowledgements

Thank you to my mentor Claudia Cortese for helping revise many of these poems in their early stages. Thank you to my fellow writers and friends Joanna Liu, Jenna Nesky, and Avery Yoder-Wells for supporting my writing throughout the creation of this chapbook. Many thanks to these magazines, in which previous versions of these poems first appeared: *The Dawn Review*, *manywor(l)ds*, *The Penn Review*, *The Rumpus*, and *diode*. I would also like to acknowledge Yehoshua November's poem "Prayer" in *Thrush Poetry Journal* for inspiring *Habitual Prayer*'s title. Finally, I would like to thank Mom, Dad, and Anna for always supporting me.

www.ingramcontent.com/pod-product-compliance
Lightning Source LLC
Chambersburg PA
CBHW070454130626
46553CB00006B/2401